Arnaud Dem

C000142251

Citroën 2 CV

The iconic deudeuche

1934 - 2017

Legend

affectionately known the Deuche France, the 2CV is one of the most recognizable icons of the country.

According to urban legend, the head of Citroën Pierre-Jules Boulanger had a brainwave a rainy afternoon in 1930 when his sparkling limousine walked behind another horse and cart by 2km / h along a muddy track.

"Why not offer to French farmers a more powerful mode of transport?" Has he said to nobody in particular.

Exceeding the lazy cart, he rushed home to reflect his innovative idea.

After doing some market research, he concluded that, by designing a robust and cheap car, he could take control of a hitherto untapped market.

A few days later, Baker told the astounded designers factory of Levallois, near Paris, the design of an "umbrella on wheels".

"And I want him to be able to carry a basket of eggs over a plowed field without breaking one," said he added.

Initially called the POS (minicar), The boss of Citroën stipulated that the vehicle had to be robust enough to cope with the country roads, consume up to three liters of petrol per 100 kilometers, be comfortable without being luxurious and require minimal maintenance.

The task was so great that it took 13 years to complete his team.

History

The work began in earnest in 1935 Michelin bought Citroën, Pierre Michelin becomes CEO and Pierre Boulanger became his deputy, Vice President and Head of Design Office.

Drom the beginning the project has been shrouded in secrecy.

As the car had to be light, the designers have experimented with corrugated panels of aircraft Junkers Ju 52 and aluminum body.

This had to be economical, so they used an engine 500cc motorcycle, and - in an attempt to combine comfort with the economy - the passengers were initially sitting in hammocks suspended from the roof by metal cables.

In 1937, the first prototype is carried away for tests in the park of an abandoned castle in La Ferte-Vidame. The tests were a disaster:

the seat hammock are braided trampolines, body rubs and chassis cracked. Back to the drawing board to the POS.

Two years later, Baker has insisted that her baby was ready to be launched.

Engineers do not agree, but now they knew discuss with the man they called "the imaginative tyrant."

Baker ordered the construction of 250 prototypes for the 1939 Motor Show.

Production began Sept. 2, 1939, but at 11 am, France and Britain declared war on Germany.

Prototype 1939

The assembly line is requisitioned for military equipment and POS under construction are scrapped ... PJB does not want his idea is echoed by the occupant.

During the long period of war, PJB works behind the scenes to his project.

The POS continues its evolution ... The Germans want to know more about his project, but he refuses any proposal. He nevertheless continued his testing.

prototype Terrasson

This prototype whose author is Pierre Terrasson, test pilot of the prototype of the 2CV from 1938 to 1939, was photographed in La Ferte-Vidame by Pierre Terrasson himself 25 August 1939.

This image is the only photograph of the prototype, the POS Project Pierre-Jules Boulanger is top secret.

This prototype was equipped with a twin engine Flat 375 cm3 water cooling whose power was 9 c.

The gearbox is made up of three speeds of which the third is overdrive. Its weight was 400 kg for a maximum speed of 70 km / h.

The "prototype 1939" is performed just after Terrasson prototype for the Paris Salon in October 1939.

It closely resembles the latter:

the only lighthouse change places, the cover is slightly modified for the adoption of the air cooling system.

All this in order to reduce the weight of the 2CV.

End of August 1939, a first series of "2CV prototype 1939" was produced 250 copies and approval mine on August 28 this year, make the "2CV prototype in 1939" a 2CV A 1939 mass produced.

But World War II marks the end of production, while studies continue discreetly.

This prototype was equipped with a twin engine Flat 375 cm3 air-cooled whose power was 9 c.

The gearbox is made up of three speeds of which the third is overdrive. Its weight was 450 kg for a maximum speed of 70 km / h.

The mysterious prototypes

Pictures taken during the project, were banned!

The test circuit was protected by blast walls, to test the car in secret day and night.

A famous photo shows the prototype with a central beacon called "Terrasson", the name of the test driver from 1938 to 1939 who took the shot three TPV La Ferte-Vidame.

**This prototype whose author is Pierre Terrasson, test pilot of the prototype of the 2CV from 1938 to 1939,
was photographed in La Ferte-Vidame August 25, 1939.
This image is the only photograph of the prototype,
POS Project Pierre-Jules Boulanger is top secret.**

The first prototype is the "pickup" that served to tire testing with Michelin, bought from a batch of scrap has been exposed to Henri Malartre museum in Rochetaillée-sur-Saône near Lyon.

The purpose of this prototype is not known today.

The second is found between 1968 and 1970 in a barn in La Ferte-Vidame, during a photo shoot. Initially destined for destruction 20 years earlier, it was dismantled and stored.

Restored, it is now good as new, and was put together by the same official tests that had protected in 1948, Henri Loridant.

However, neither the prototype nor Terrasson "Cyclops", the name of this proto 1942 profiled central lighthouse, have been found.

Pick up transformed Michelin 1937

First prototype "pickup" that served to tire testing for Michelin which was bought from a batch of scrap has been exposed to Henri Malartre museum in Rochetaillée-sur-Saône, near Lyon.

The discovery of three 2CV prototype in the attic of the farm of the Center of La Ferte-Vidame tests.

In 1994, Jean-Claude sends Lannes with a colleague and a truck to recover the equipment Test Center located in Eure-et-Loir.

Upon leaving, the maintenance manager of the premises said:

"There are still parts 2CV in attics".

Intrigued, they go up in the sub-slope and realize three cars, hidden under tarps.

They raise them: each is a 2CV prototype.

Complete cars, certainly not in exceptional condition (the sheet metal are damaged), but for 2CV prototypes is already amazing!

Only in 1998 for the 50th anniversary of the 2CV those three relics are presented to the public (Rétromobile in Paris).

There are no plans to restore them, they are kept in the state by the Citroën Conservatoire.

the Cyclops

1942

There is no 2CV Cyclops period, just sketches, the first date of 1942, and the following 1946 and 1947.

However, there is a photo of the prototype, taken in 1948 by a journalist who takes his shot over the boundary wall of the test center of La Ferte-Vidame.

This photograph published in the daily "La Presse", in 1948, just months before the release of the final model.

We can therefore deduce that Cyclops served mule Citroen, the final version of Salon is quite different.

This prototype named "Cyclops" because the only light is placed at cover center, is made in 1942 (the laying of two lighthouses was not mandatory at the time).

Pierre-Jules Boulanger wanted some body elements pressed steel, this model 1942 there are very few forms and use a lot of sharp corners.

Many changes are made, the first road tests begin.
She was nicknamed "Cyclops" because of its unique lighthouse.

For the record, from the lighthouse was placed in the hood center.

But at night, we quickly realized that other vehicles coming from the front, brushed body, thinking it was a motorcycle.
The lighthouse has been placed on the left of the car.

The "Cyclops" also has a Flat Twin engine 375 cm3 air-cooled whose power was 9 c.

The gearbox is made up of three speeds of which the third is overdrive.

Its weight was 450 kg for a maximum speed of 70 km / h.

In 1946, the shape of the Cyclops prototype changes and becomes increasingly close to the final 2CV.

But Pierre-Jules Boulanger being refractory to stamping wings refuses this proposal.

Prototype
1946

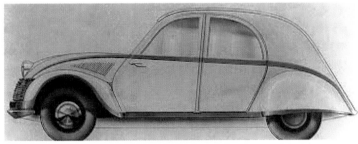

This Cyclops prototype 1947 is also of growing closer to the final 2CV.

Prototype
1947

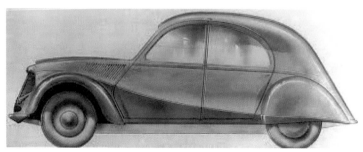

On both Cyclops, the large width of the front grille shows the abandonment of cooling water for the engine air cooling.

TPV, now christened 2CV 1948

When peace came in 1945, Baker dragged the only prototype of its POS, remained hidden in a loft in La Ferte-Vidame, and invited Flaminio Bertoni, the man who later created another legend the Citroën DS.

Following some problems start, we abandon the "thread starter" (mower type grass). now placed there a battery and an electric starter.

In October 1948, the car is presented at the Salon before the astonished eyes of the public ... When the cover is removed, people pushing, shoving ... Everyone wants to see.

The car was unveiled secret ... except its engine. The hood, welded, does not see it.

Opinions are divided ... Some think a joke and others see this car as an object of escape ...

Gradually, as the days of the show happen, other manufacturers start laughing "yellow" ... Citroen managed to "touch" the audience ...

She is the queen Fair !!!

2CV - AT

1949

Finally, after many changes and lead a standard model June 24, 1949 Finally, a successful 2CV is received by the approval authority of Mines, pursuant to a request made by the Quai de Javel three days earlier.

This is the car with the chassis number 0001.

The 2CV is identical to those that will be built a few weeks later at the factory in Levallois.

2CV named A, it is equipped with an engine of 375 cm3.

Only four vehicles are manufactured each day to cope with the growing demand.

As planned by Pierre Jules Boulanger, the 2CV is designed for businesses that require frequent travel. A dossier supporting use of the vehicle must be entered!

But that's not all ... the "happy" 2CV owners are asked to give their impressions after a few months always with the aim of continually improving.

More and more people want a 2CV and the delivery time is seven years ....

The production start-up, the first customers handpicked could place orders.

Those lucky however must be patient and wait 3 to 5 years before receiving delivery of the 2CV.

Indeed, the demand for more and more important over the weeks quickly extended the delivery time, the plant up to a rate likely to serve everyone.

Pierre-Jules Boulanger will celebrate the success of his car.

He will find death in 1950 in a road accident during testing a prototype of the VDG, the future DS.

This 2CV 1949, awarded in January 2018 to 75,600 euros.

It is now the most expensive 2CV whole story.

2CV - AU
1950

The production is accelerating (400 units per day) and the number of 2CV driving on the roads of France grows.

It is found in many trades (social workers, rural doctors, factors, priests, etc ...).

At the 1950 Salon, Citroen offers a van release.

The crowd gathers and orders flow.

This is a commercial vehicle expected by the population.

It is named 2CV IN

(U as utility).

1951

The van is now available for sale.

On multiple uses, it is popular in the fields of delivery.

You have to be very patient to acquire hers because the waiting lists can be several years ...

It is not uncommon for people who receive their AU recommend another immediately to be sure of having a 5 or 6 years later!

In 1951, the 2CV is presented to PTT.

Tests with the sedan version called series "Type A" are carried Savernes in the Lower Rhine in 1952.

Responding to the engine targets rural tours, these trials are successful and validate in fact the entrance to the 2CV in the postal vehicle fleet.

2CV - AZU positions

1952

In 1952 appears the van Post in its green livery.

Auxiliary French factors, other 2CV vans will be used by various technical services positions.

Appreciated for its simplicity and robustness, the AZU 2CV was used as the official vehicle for the posts of many European countries.

The first 2CV vans are delivered in gray, since Citroën has not planned another painting system.

Normally the material Post Office should nevertheless take the regulatory livery, dark green with the inscriptions "Post" in yellow letters.

But this requirement quickly becomes too expensive after a few copies painted green, the Post 2CV will therefore be all painted gray.

Until 1962 and finally they receive a yellow livery ... to the delight of our eyes.

2CV Pierre Barbot

1953

Built in the unit between 1951 and 1953, the 2CV Barbot will at the highest color and Citroën 2CV.

Created by a physical-chemical engineer and led by a young prodigy (Jean Vinatier), the tray will run much ink.

Shortened 25cm compared to the original 2CV, each of the tray component member must be adjusted, adapted or remanufactured.

Only the wings will be kept original, except the integration of headlights in the wings.

She will arrive victorious at the Golden Bowl in 1953, pulverizing the record of 24 hours.

Changing grille

1953

Changing the type of grille.

The circle was removed, leaving only the two major aluminum rafters.

The hole for the crank is always present.

**grille Oval
before 1953**

From 1953

2CV Dagonet

1953/1956

In the 1950s, the success of the 2CV is such that everyone wants to go to its special version.

After spending long hours in his studio, Mr Jean Dagonet his dream by changing the engine of 2 CV (with the original displacement of the smaller engine 375 cm3 to 425 cm3) and the body a few years later.

Between 1953 and 1957, Jean will offer several bodies including that of 1956.

John will have, for personal vehicle, a contoured Dagonet for speed and with additional lighthouses, whitewall tires and a race number.

Another part in the famous Italian race Mille Miglia in 1955.

Citroën 2CV Dagonet 1956

2CV Dagonet (phase 3), 1956.

That year, the final version of the 2CV Dagonet has a fiberglass body.

Citroën 2CV model Dagonet sheeted

2CV - PO

1954

wavy covers

Beginning in 1954 appears on the catalog Citroën 2CV a model, called PO with reinforced equipment to meet a specification of specific loads:

driving outside France on difficult roads of overseas territories.

2CV PO (for "Dust") to protect the motor from the sand.

2CV - AZ

In October 1954, Citroën presents a new 2CV:

type AZ. More powerful than the type A, it now develops 12 hp for 9 against its predecessor.

Extra power still significant, especially in more self inaugurates a new technology on the 2CV: the centrifugal clutch.

Basically, this is a clutch that automatically engages below 1000 rev / min, which makes use of the 2CV more pleasant city.

With the centrifugal clutch 2CV actually adopts a kind of automatic transmission.
You had dreamed, Citroen did!

Besides performance, the 2CV AZ does not differ in any of the 2CV Type A which is the basis, both cars being exactly identical.
To adapt to the new safety standards, all 2CV sedan receiving side indicators.

Also in the area of security, the speedometer is now illuminated.

Practical detail, before the impressive number of drivers who have broken elbow (when it was not the fingers ...) with the inadvertent dropping of the half-glass front, Citroen finally decides to install a clip to hold the window.

While its effectiveness is relative, but that's something ...

A U 2CV model is mounted in the Forest Plants in Belgium.

There is a rear trunk, bumper purposes, a trapezoidal window, lights on the wings, "alloy" disk wheels, chrome strips for decoration and wing hooves, etc ...

2CV - AZL

In 1956 in France, there is no need to know the 2CV, which never ceases to seduce.

With L as Deluxe, the 2CV AZL stands 2CV A and AZ by new development inside and outside.

Turning to an optimized finishing, wheels, bumpers, the metal frame of the seats and the shifter ball adorn a light shade.

polished aluminum rods adorn the rocker, the middle cover and contours of the bumper.

Shades such as blue, green or burgundy appear in the cockpit.

Michelin 2CV

1954

Owner of the firm since 1935 Citroën, Michelin is at the origin of the project 2CV.

The success of the 2CV (AZU, AU and sedan) makes it an ideal vehicle for the tire manufacturer's fleet, which will be equipped as 1954, 2CV truck for nearly 20 years.

iconic character Michelin tires, which constitute his body, Bibendum is known worldwide and is proud to be, since a distinction received in 2000, the best logo of the century.

There are several versions, but the truck cab for plastic Bibendum remains popular.

CAPE TOWN - OSLO - MONTE CARLO
1953

When Michèle Bernier decided to embark on the adventure with Jacques DUVEY, they are convinced that they will achieve a feat ...

Indeed, they will cross the continent from Cape Town to Algiers (about 18,000 km) and it will be the first to cross the Sahara 2CV!

They then join Oslo, Norway, starting point of the 7th Monte Carlo Rally.

A 2CV from the Monte Carlo Rally, it makes smile.

They then pass the finish line on time, at the 323rd spot.

Their 2CV "A" thus enters into the history of heroic ads Citroen and make good figure.

AZLP

1957

This new 2CV, AZLP model series (L for Luxury and P for Gate Malle) therefore includes, for the first time a door trunk manufactured by Citroen.

It is hinged under the rear window, provides sufficient opening and is equipped with a lock closure.

trunks bulging

Among the original features of the first 2CV ... his coat which serves both roof and trunk door, down to the rear registration plate.

Concept clever, economical but not always satisfactory to the owners ... it's doors and various trunk appear quickly.

They are initially flat, then some curved models are needed ... which increases the boot capacity.

Malle self-access

preserving its original registration.

The rear trunk encompassing e pressed the car

piece of steel.

Malle and Courbevoie maintaining registration original.

Malle and Courbevoie big model.

**Malle curved back
Type "Raoul"**

Malle speed

fixing on sheet reported

under rear window.

Malle pecazaux

Malle Guilleman record

Malle Blondin Neuilly

**Malle ER large
interior gutter
hidden under the canvas.**

Gate trunk

DOG

Malle S.MA.RTS

allows an opening

total of the rear bay.

commercial two gates

AG Record

Rare opening

Guilleman

1957

of the top fabric of the descent is
replaced by a box sheet.

Trunk / Tailgate

Taxi AZLP

1957

Following the oil crisis during the summer of 1956, it focuses on small-displacement cars.

Given the simplicity of the 2CV and fuel rationing caused by the crisis of the Suez Canal, the direction of Quai de Javel believes that there is a market potential of the project for taxi transport.

In 1957 Citroën 2CV offers our National Taxi release.

A seat for the driver, no passenger seat (folded into the box).

The client remains in the rear seat, with the option to extend his legs.

AZLP World Tour

1958

2CV Seguela Baudot - Sarthe Museum

First car to have performed around the world, from October 1958 to November 1959.

Jean-Claude Baudot and Jacques Séguéla traveled more than 100,000 km in 400 days at the wheel of their AZLP 2CV and made back the little Citroën in history.

80,000 kms by car and more than 20,000 boat. 100 000 km in total in 13 months (250 kms per day) 50 countries - 5 continents.

Citroneta Chile

1959

In ChileCitroën Chilena SA was born in 1959 thanks to its plant in Arica.

It will be the first in South America to assemble the 2CV and its exceptional driving qualities experiencing a popular fad.

But the Chilean Citroneta is almost a strange 2CV, with a body unusual three volumes.

A pick-up and a break Citroneta complement the range from 1963 and the adventure ends in 1974.

2CV "Sahara"

The history of the 2CV Sahara does not start in the Quai de Javel of design offices, but in the Landes where a M.Bonnafous engineer in public works, looking from 1954 vehicle all- land for business purposes.

At that time, the Jeep was the ultimate off-road, but spare parts were expensive and sometimes hard to find.

Bored, he was looking for a similar vehicle but that is also economical, lightweight and reliable; but the automotive market certainly nothing like it.

Therefore, M.Bonnafous decided to design the vehicle he sought, he took as a basis the Citroën 2CV. Logic, it was the cheapest car on the market, the simplest and therefore the easiest to tinker.

Only downside, the order books were full for the 2CV to the early 1950s, suggesting that M.Bonnafous already had a 2CV, unless he bought a used copy.

On this basis, M.Bonnafous will do crafts.

Instead of realizing a four-wheel drive, it decides that a second motor on the 2CV positioned in the trunk.

Thus, each motor drives the axle, with the ability to switch to two-wheel drive axle, leaving a "free wheel".

Also, the two motors at the ends of the car allow weight distribution, an advantage in the steep paths.

For simplicity, both engines are independent of each other, and each has its gearbox, its starter and even his tank ...

The tanks just as the engine takes place in the trunk, the tank can no longer accommodate it. M.Bonnafous however is a good place for them:

under the front seats! Smoking, refrain from a smoke on board! Also, to fill the two tanks of 15 liters each, you had to open the doors ... inconvenient to the obvious. But that does not stop at M.Bonnafous produce two Twin 2CV for his company between 1954 and 1955.

From a small handyman Landes for marketing by Citroen, there is a gap that M.Bonnafous never thought passable even by 2CV Twin.

Yet Citroën heard of this joyful yourself and it will pay close attention given the performance all terrain attributed to him.

Recall that in mid-1950, it is the black gold rush in Algeria, the oil companies are then looking for equipment able to face the dunes of the Sahara. But also, such a product might be interested in the administration, and why not individuals.

Thus, Citroën build prototypes on the model of the twin-engine 2CV Bonnafous, and tests the Ermenonville sand sea.

The first of them is ready in March 1958, he is recognized by his body still very close to the series of 2CV, with a trunk door having a very small air inlet, and which did not close the Because of the engine space.

These first tests are promising, so Citroën began to develop the model.

To improve the cooling of the rear motor, it generates a substantial indentation in the trunk so that the fan can take come directly from the air; and we cut some vents in the quarter for this purpose.

The ideas are good and will be gradually refined to go to the production model.

A second prototype is then constructed during the second half of 1958 to be at the show utility that takes place in November.

Then a third prototype was presented in July 1959 in the French army, after a long development.

If the army does not hold this car to enter the ranks, that does not stop to present the car to the public in September 1959 under the name "2CV Sahara".

The specifications of the car at what interest:

2CV Sahara pairs of twins who develop 13CH 425cm3 each fed by a carburetor Solex 26 CBIN kind (oil bath air filter optional).

If the car has two gearboxes, they work simultaneously by a hydraulic control that operates both clutches simultaneously.

Each engine has a generator to charge the battery ...

body side, the 2CV Sahara is unmistakable with its spare wheel placed on the hood to the way Land Rover, its specific rear or rear wings notched.

But the 2CV Sahara is primarily crafts, such as rear fenders are widened and cut from standard 2CV wings, a simple plate welded butcher comes the location of the chute for example. But the car also is not practical, as the front doors cut to allow filling of the tank without having to open them.

As for the capabilities of the car, the 2CV Sahara can roll up to 110km / h on the condition of having two engines in action, failing that, the weight of an engine idle just cripple performance.

Consumption side, Citroen advanced between 9 and 12 liters per 100km with both engines. And crossing side, the 2CV Sahara was quite efficient, able to go where other cars did not dare to venture.

The marketing and began in December 1960, production starts in the Panhard factory Ivry.

But the 2CV Sahara is proposed to double the price of a basic 2CV, limiting its spread throughout his career.

Quickly, Citroën organized a small event to demonstrate the capabilities of the car, in July 1961 a 2CV Sahara climbs on the Dune du Pyla in four hours.

But in 1962, France lost Algeria and the Sahara 2CV loses its main market.

To avoid incurring the resentment of the independence of this former French region Citroën changes the name of the car that becomes 2CV 4 × 4.

In 1964, the 2CV Sahara was also produced in Spain in duplicate with the Ivry plant, and that same year, the front doors open in the right direction as the rest of the range.

In the end, sales remain anecdotal and Citroën puts an end to the adventure in 1967 after 693 copies produced.

A mystery remains, one 674th of a copy which was assembled in 1971

...

The 60s

the decade of renewal

From December 1960 change in tone:

new hood 5 ribs, each air intake side and new completely redesigned light alloy calender.

The 2CV AZ 375cc model disappears from the catalog and new colors appear:

spray green, yellow panama hat, blue steel.

The Radioën meanwhile appeared in the cockpit as the first radio station available for a 2CV.

DThe wheels 400 are replaced by wheels 380.

2CV Argentina

1960

In Argentina(To Catila) in 1960 was a 2CV meeting with big bumpers and a third side window with spare parts from Levallois.

Agreements were signed in 1971 with Inda SA in Paraguay and Uruguay and Quinatar SA Avils Algaro in Ecuador for local assembly 2CV and 3 HP.

The 2CV 6 (602cm3 equipped with an engine of 26ch to 29ch) is called 3HP Argentina (602cm3 displacement to 32CH).

The history of the 2CV in Argentina spans more than twenty years with a total output of 220 + 000 vehicles (8 Break Ami, Mehari and included vans, including about 77,000 for 3HP).

From February 1960 to April 1961, the AZL and the hood AZU "Corrugated sheet" are assembled with components from the plant Forest.

Hence the current expression in Argentina to 2CV "Belgian hood".

Note that the Argentine 2CV come with big bumpers, otherwise the wings and the bonnet are stamped in parking lots by the bumper much higher for Ford and other American cars long trunk that prevented the visibility to 'back.

The last 2CV was released from the chains of Barracas district of Buenos Aires in 1972.

After the departure of Citroën, an Argentine manufacturer resumed production of 3HP and Mehari in the 1980s with some models like the IES America and named pickup IES Gringa.

IES America

van 1961

The van adopt amendments of the sedan.

New colors available:

blue with sea blue interior, with red poppy red interior (dark brown or gray top).

Mixed 2CV 1962

Arrival of a new model dubbed the Joint 2CV. For Belgium, it took the name 2CV AZC (C for "Commercial").

Special opening for the trunk (the rear window also notes with overall), to load larger objects ..
 original thing, the spare wheel is fixed under the hood

2CV AZAM - 1963

This 2CV AZAM is a "2CV AZ-improved".

She is the first 2CV to feature enhancements comfort and elegance.

The seats of the Friend 6 come equip 2CV improving comfort, polished aluminum rods adorn the cover (5 ribs), the rocker, the windscreen bay, the joints of windows and windscreens -chocs.

bumper bananas are they replaced with loop-shaped chrome tubes.

Also borrowed from the Ami 6, chrome hubcaps are emerging.

Other features:

two hoods, the seat frames fabric is red, the steering wheel is white bakelite and the ceiling is round.

The colors available for sale are green Embrun (replaced by Agave Green in September 1964), beige Antilleans (replaced by gray Typhoon in September 1963 itself replaced by the Etna gray in June 1965), the slate blue (replaced by the blue Monte Carlo 1964).

In 1964, the Avants seatbelts become ventral and disappear central scouts license plates.

Another new hammock object holder is stretched between the backrest of the rear seat and the fixing of the trunk door.

On the dashboard, the trapezoidal speedometer overlooks a fuel gauge.

The flashing column is now attached to the steering column and the starter takes place under the vacuum pockets left of the steering wheel.

The pull of the starter it takes place below the central pockets quickly, level shifter.

1965

In 1965 comes a new grille with three horizontal blades.

The rafters are moved a little further up the hood (5 ribs).
The model is called AZL AZA in the sales catalog.
New colors: blue and gray Fog Etna.
A new side window, called side window is added.

1967

The 2CV AZAM is renamed Export.

2CV4 / 2CV6

1970

beginning 1970, The range of 2 CV is modified and is now divided into two models:

2 CV 4 equipped with a 435 cm 3 of 24 c (at 6750 rev / min) having not much to do with the 425 cm3d'antan and 2 CV 6 equipped with a 602 hp 29 cm3 close to that of the Ami 6.

The only thing that differentiates the 2cv4 2cv6 is the logo on the trunk door because these two models are very close indeed.

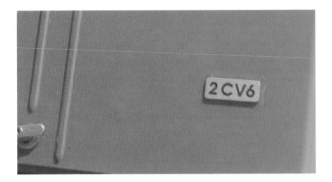

It will be a key contact and steering lock on the steering column but the start will be made on pushing a red button on the dashboard until 1974.

It will have rectangular flashing orange until May 1970.

This was also the case on the French model.

In France there has been so for a few months, the same rectangular flashing those who were mounted on Belgian 2CV from 1961 to 1970.

Flower-Power

1970

The hippie movement, born in California in the mid 60s, reached Europe a few years later and delights drive only through one type of model:

2CV. The car is presented, "Peace & Love" 1970, symbolizes the heyday of the small Citroen, like its slogan of the time "More than a car, it's a lifestyle," the latter summarized very well the 2CV Flower Power.

THE RAIDS IN 2CV

Men and women continue to live in the myth of the first Citroën raids by offering 2CV travels around the world.

Organizers for which some have been opportunity to participate in these mythical raids Citroën seventy years.

ADVENTURE 2CV
OF SEVENTY YEARS:

THE RAID Citroën PARIS-PARIS-KABUL

1970

Given the enthusiasm of young people to try their luck in a 2CV Citroen organizes its first raid, from 1 to 29 August 1970, the Paris-Kabul-Paris or 16,500 km, with the participation of the Ministry of Youth and Sports.

The raid is open to all young people under 30 with their 2CV, Diane or camel.

5000 Citroen lists inquiries, 1200 535 pre-registrations and registrations farms.

At the time Afghanistan was sort of Mecca of independent adventurers.

It is therefore natural that the city of Kabul is chosen as the destination.

Paris will see 494 teams or 1,300 young people from this great adventure.

Participants are free to choose their path, but must respect groupings in place and time data throughout the course.

On arrival in Kabul there were 480 crews including 364 on time.

And on the return, Paris will have 458 teams including 320 and 213 in time without any driving penalties.

THE RAID Citroën PARIS-PARIS-PERSEPOLIS

1971

1971 Raid Paris-Persepolis-Paris

Given the success of the first raid, Citroën decided to do it again with a Paris-Persepolis-Paris. A ballad of 13,500 km of 31 July to 31 August 1971.

This year 500 teams involved in the adventure, always with the same conditions of age, between 18 and 30 years.

The classification as the previous year, based on the control points, the allotted time, but also on the overall condition of the car when they return and documents (photos and soundtracks) reported the trip.

THE RAID THE CITROËN GRAN Traversia

1972

After the first two raids Citroen France, the craze is emulated. On the other side of the Atlantic, is Citroën Argentina organizes its first major raid.

A loop of 28 days nearly 11,000 km between Buenos Aires - Land of Fire - Santiago - Buenos Aires.

From January 31 to February 27, 1972, nearly 256 crews 2CV, 3 HP, van, camel and AMI 8 go on an adventure in this extraordinary expedition.

As for Citroen France raids, the rules are the same:

respect for waypoints and time hours, and photographic reports, audio or monographic.

2CV Rally

1973

Abidjan Party October 29, 1973, the 2CV through Black Africa with his tricky runs, its mud, its fords, then comes the Sahara with the great crossing of the Ténéré.

This will then Djado the Taffassasset, the rise of Assekrem in Hoggar, the long climb back to Tunisia by the Tans-Saharan Africa and finally the official arrival in Marseilles on 1 December 1973.

It was at the initiative of Jacques Wolgensinger, Head of Citroën's communication department, the project was born.
100 young people from 18 to 30 years, including 8 women, are divided into 60 crews.

Among the 4894 candidates in 1000 will be selected on record.

They will determined at a weekend at the Halles de Paris, Rungis and in the end there will be only 100.

2CV Palmeraie

1973

Green Palmeraie (AC529) was a Citroën shade available just one year, from July 1973 to September 1974 on the 2CV.

The 2CV come with this particular shade received a harlequin upholstery fabrics.

Changing grille

1974

Small rafters, who were on the cover, slide again on the grille.

It will have the grille 3 branches until 1974 or it will be the new plastic grille, roof cover will disappear.

The hood now opens from the inside, plastic headbands facilitating the opening of the doors.

A big change :

the arrival of rectangular headlights.

2CV Spot

1976

The 2CV SPOT was created in 1976 by Serge Gevin.

It is billed as the first production
special series in France.

Its colors are very trendy at the time, then it was something out of
"Fun" for the time!

A first attempt for Citroën, suddenly Master.

With 1,800 copies sold, we can really talk about the "first limited
series".

Spot The 2CV has a specific and recognizable among a thousand delivered, it is the work of young designer Serge Gevin who offers him a white livery and orange, two shades in the tone of the time.

All, however, remains fairly simple, the idea is to give a "vacationer" mind this 2CV since originally the project was to give birth to a "2CV Transat", but the term "Spot" was preferred.

2CV Basketball

1977

In the fall of 1976, students of second year of the Camondo school are offered by their teacher Carlos Caceres, with the support of Warden Henry Malvaux, a contest to study graphic and chromatic solutions specific to individualize an industrial product of general circulation.

The 2CV has been chosen as a basis, the service Citroen PR provides them with all the elements necessary for their work.

Of the 50 projects developed, two are made in 1977 by Citroën on real cars.

The manufacturer thus gives life to a copy of the 2CV blue, white and black designed by Loïc Le Sabazec and Stéphane Jean, as well as two copies of the 2CV Basketball designed by Claire Pagniez.

The winner defined his project as follows:

"To express the young and adventure of the 2CV side, I immediately rejected the pure graphics.

I thought of the basketball shoe or tennis, carried by all American youth, often flabby and distorted after long journeys by hitchhiking or walking. "

It symbolizes the idea that we have of the 2CV:

the car you buy for twenty years and with which one undertakes a little crazy trips we never remake.

It was sold only at 2 copies, not surprising that we see no trace.

It will inspire the model marketed in Spain:

Marcatello the 2CV.

1978/1979

From September 1978 the car found the third ice (the quarter), significantly reducing the blind spot.

Finally, in July 1979, the 435 cc engine was abandoned and now all 2CV Special feature the 602 cm³ of 2CV6.

It becomes the special 2CV6 and 2CV6 2CV6 comfort becomes the club.

2cv6 Club (left) and Special (right)

2CV - 6 Special E 1981

Another surprising return, that of the centrifugal clutch! To meet a growing demand from city dwellers, Citroën decided to update the equipment that had been somewhat forgotten since the 1960s.

In May 1981 therefore appears the 2cv6 Special E. E is naturally centrifugal clutch.

Practical, this version does not attract the crowds. Comparable in all respects to the Special 2cv6 which it derives, the Special E does is distinguished only by his surname, proudly displayed on the trunk door.

First interested townspeople are meanwhile tired of the heavy direction of the 2CV and now demand more compact models, more modern, more comfortable as the Renault 5.

Moreover, oddly enough Citroën does little to communicate on this model, preferring to highlight popular models like Charleston.

Very discreet commercially, the Special E disappear in July 1983.

Citroen 2CV Charleston

(1980-1981)

In the late 70s, sales of 2CV erode.

The clientele is increasingly drawn to more modern cars, more compact, less rudimentary.

Especially young customers may turn away from the 2CV accusing thirty years, despite the many made to date since 1948.

This is to attract this target only limited to 8000 copies series is imagined.

It is then energize the 2CV by an attractive package.

This is Serge Gevin is responsible design.

A painting two-tone wife the outline of the top door to return to the front wing in a rounded and elegant curved also highlighted by a gray liserai.

The two colors used are black and red Delage, known for its warmth and elegance.

The wheels are also painted red and chrome trim Dyane 6 comes enhance the color.

The headlights are painted red, as well as the contour of the windshield.

Inside is a 2CV Club with benches separated front overlaid with a fabric "foot-cock".

The engine is one of the 2CV 6, ie 602 cm3 of 29 hp.

Presented at the Motor Show 1980 (which was not called yet "Mondial de l'Automobile"), the new "nice car" sensation. The name evokes the Charleston crazy years (1920-1930), painted on the door of trunk right side, is a success.

Especially the presentation on the Citroën stand sensation with an escort of young ladies wearing fashionable roaring twenties, wearing pearl short dresses, frills and cigarette holders.

So the 2CV Charleston a hit and 8,000 copies of the limited edition, though more expensive by almost 10% as the 2CV Club, and 25% more than the 2CV Special.

She pulls the entire range up so that two decisions were taken:

stopping the production is delayed, and Charleston is integrated into the ordinary range in July 1981 (1982 vintage).

The 1981 Charleston knows some differences with the limited series.

At first glance you will notice the chrome headlights and not painted red Delage.

The first models retain the same inscription on the door of the trunk, but soon the monogram "2CV Charleston" will be affixed on the left side in chrome letters on black, like all of the Citroën range.

Inside, the seats abandon the "foot-cock" for upholstery gray plain fabric tiles.

2CV 007

nineteen eighty one

A year after the Charleston, the fate 2CV 007 to mark mediatically prowess of a 2CV used by Roger Moore and Carole Bouquet in a mad chase in Spain, in the film For Your Eyes Only.

This film was finishing 2CV Club with a strengthened and a 4-cylinder engine chassis, but the typical noise of the 2CV has been preserved thanks to a special exhaust.

First presented in England, the 2CV 007 out of 500 in right-hand drive, then in France to 500 copies.

The 007 is a 2CV 6 Special yellow with black adhesive patterns including registration 007, 7 being coupled with a gun, on the doors, hood and trunk door.

Special interesting, the car comes with, on the dashboard, a bag of stickers reproducing revolver bullet holes, to glue itself on the car, so that the 2CV 007 could be customized!

This is the only 2CV Charleston to receive the color Yellow Helios.

The inside was that of the special 2CV without any addition ie bench toe black ventilated, no passenger visor sun, small counter.

The only analogy to the model that was used for the film is rectangular headlights.

The cars are well delivered at a rate of one per dealer, only for promotion.

The presentation of the first models of this series takes place in the company of actors of the film on the Place Vendome in October 1981.

Although the waterfall was made by Rémy Julienne, three 2CV 6 used for filming were prepared by Ken Shepard, British stuntman known of the early 80s.

The vehicles were shipped by Paris Citroën factory in Slough, England, and then to the garage Ken Shepard. The,

the 2CV suffered many changes (engine, chassis, exhaust, arches ...)

Two cars were used for the waterfall, the third only served at filming interior scenes.

Ken Shepard manufactured a prototype that was never used and destroyed.

Charleston Eligor

1982

The goal is to attract a different clientele, less attracted by the spirit "Roaring Twenties".

The royal blue is dynamic and assembly hues successful.
If blue is a color that appeals to many, it is difficult to accurately identify to whom, and therefore to quantify the hoped for sales.

This is probably why a bright yellow tagged "younger" will eventually be preferred.

questionable choice if we are to believe the sales made with Charleston Helios yellow and black, which also succeed another classic hue, a year later, based on gray.

Today, it remains to collectors happiness to enjoy the rare side of the yellow model ... while dreaming of hypothetical blue!

Charleston 1982

In 1982, the Charleston offer a variant.

It is possible to abandon the red Delage for a yellow "Helios", very showy.

If the red Delage seduced by its elegance, yellow Helios swore and was as a foil.

Faced with this failure, Citroën react fast!

It will remain one year to the catalog.

That makes today a sought after model collectors saw fewer sales !!!

It becomes a model of the most copied seen its rarity ...

Marcatelo 1982

Spain

Special series for the Hispanic market 2CV Marcatelo takes a winning idea in France in 1976:

Basketball the 2CV, the grimant Deuche in athletic shoe. In 1982, Spain holds the world championship football. Originally scheduled to 500 copies, the 2CV Marcatelo will eventually produced 300 copies.

Echoing the bright colors of holding football team players from Spain, the 2CV Marcatelo is made from the most common Spanish model, the 2CV 6 CT (French Special a few things about), corresponding to the entry level.

To the chagrin of collectors, Marcatelo 2CV adhesives used on a majority of the body, these stickers easily lose their color in the sun.

Each copy is numbered product separately to the left of the trunk door. Right, she wears a "2CV 82" logo.

Inside the car, the seats are covered with a striped orange fabric unevenly black and red, with orange plastic sides.

charleston
1983

From July 1983 a new version Charleston born.

Citroën catches up and takes a more sober style.

Sober is not the ideal term, say "classic".

A light gray (gray cormorant), associated with a Midnight Silver.
This model will remain until the end of the catalog.

A difference with previous models:

the hue of its wheels is granted with that of
bumper and not with the body color.

2CV France 3

1983

Early 80s:

production of the 2CV passes under the symbolic 100 000.

To maintain sales, Citroën will launch every year from 1983 to 1986 for France a limited series a bit like the Charleston and the success was immediate.

Apart from the 2CV 007 (end 1981), the production was confidential at the time of the limited series continues with the 2CV France 3.

It's a formula that has already been tested with the range of twins:

2CV Spot (1977), Dyane Caban (1977), 2CV Charleston (1980) and with the GS Basalt (1978) and Visa Sextant (1980) and that appeals to customers.

Citroën sponsors then the French yacht France 3 participating in the America's Cup in Newport.

On each sale of 2CV France 3, a sum was to return to the maintenance of the yacht France 3 (500 francs).

It is for once a little far from the world automotive as stated by the Director of Public Relations Jacques Wolgensinger which was not favorable to such sponsorship.

In the process, in April 1983 Citroën 2CV out a navy atmosphere based 2CV Special:

2CV France 3. It was conducted by RSCG.

It is white with blue waves on the doors, blue stripes on the hood, trunk and hood door.

She receives a specific upholstery always in the same spirit; blue door panels and seats white with blue stripes.

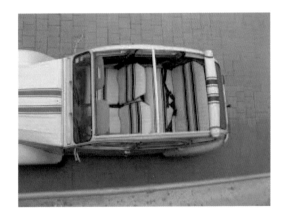

flashing brackets are gray.

2000 copies are made for France 3 but success is not at the appointment contrary to Charleston.

After the event, Citroën still has many France 3 in concessions.

An advertising document "Forward France 3! "Duplex has been published for the occasion.

En avant France 3!

White and blue, here the 2CV France 3, a limited series that will rally all the votes of supporters of the French Challenge for the America's Cup. "

2CV Adventure

1983

This is not a limited edition, but a set of body parts available accessory that can give a "look adventurer" on small Citroen.

Kit contents:
The following items can be purchased separately.
The installation of certain elements can be quite tricky (cutting the wings in particular).

The complete kit is referenced: ZC 9867216 U.

- Tubular front bumper with grilles (replaces the serial bumper and fits the original fittings). Using the handle requires the extension. - Rear carrier ("Veronica") on tailgate. - tubular rear bumper (replaces the serial bumper and fits the original fittings). - Rear carrier ("Veronica") on tailgate. - tubular rear bumper (replaces the serial bumper and fits the original fittings). - Protection mesh headlights. - Set of four external handles on the body.

Citroën spring in France 3

1984

There is no boat race but this time it's the feeling of recreation that will be the leitmotif and selling point.

This time, it is broadcast for export under different names:

Transat for Germany, Spain, Austria and the Netherlands and Beachcomber for Great Britain.

As the name Transat (taken from the prototype of the Spot) actually evokes holidays, seaside Beachcomber means of wrecks pickup which is not very complimentary.

There are some minor differences between the models finish but the exterior appearance is the same.

The boat will only be present on the trunk door of the French model.

The same advertising material as that of 1983 was reprinted for this series in 1984.

2CV Transat

Charleston Special series

1984

In 1984, the grille is surrounded by a black circle instead of chrome, whatever the color of the car and the windscreen surround is painted black (or gray Nocturne).

The color wheel is no longer accorded with the color of the car, but with the color of the bumper (or light gray).

Charleston Special series 1984

Nocturne Gray / Gray Cormorant.

Fireball 2CV / Switzerland

1985

Model exclusively for the Swiss. In the style of American sports very aggressive look, the 2CV is red with yellow flames coming out of the engine.

A special series that appears humorous when one knows the character "very athletic" 2 CV!

The basis of this is a 2 CV 2 CV 6 Special red Geranium (AC 435) having round headlights and a strapping chrome plastic grille.

Besides the flames laterally out of the hood, there is also a ball of fire on the hood and the trunk lid.

The seats are covered with fabrics striped beige and brown similar to those installed in the 2CV club of the same period. These fabrics were also optional on the 2 CV 6 Special.

The number 2 HP Fireball is not known with certainty but must be reduced to a few hundred.

It seems that the humor in this series did not please many people and some of them would have been sold without the stickers.

Grün-Ente (Duck Green)

Germany / Switzerland

1985

The 2CV has always been the darling of the green Germans and Swiss.

In 1985 it is their favorite vehicle, because it still runs on unleaded gasoline, the German and Swiss importers benefit to start Ente Grün-series, which becomes Green Duck in Switzerland.

The decoration on the doors is near Charleston, except that everything is ecological color.

A duck that flies on the front door by proudly wearing an aviator hat said to those who admire:

"I fly Bleifrei" I fly unleaded.

The Anglo-German barbarism will not be changed on the Swiss model, but in French

Unknown Production!

2CV Paris airports

1985

The 2CV entered the fleet in 1954 Paris airports.

It comes, then, become embedded in a park already made by Citroën H Van and vehicles of other makes. In the archives of ADP, there is also the transition from a Traction Avant 11 CV.

Despite legislation that imposes the color yellow, 2 CV A, first to enter the scene, retains its original gray paint.

The following, however, will the standards imposed by ADP. 2 CV will ensure its service on the tarmac until 1990, as an assistance vehicle, transportation or intervention.

She will be joined by AKS 400, the 2 CV 4 and the Ami 8 commercial break. This is the AX that will replace it. tint thereafter.

We also found some white 2 CV siglées ADP for specific missions, such as Coordinator or inter-airport moving vehicle.

Dolly
1985/1986

This limited edition is original in its composition:

it has in fact seven different versions made in three successive series.

1st series: (March 21, 1985): 3,000 copies, including 1,500 in France.
2nd series: (October 1985): 2000 copies, 600 for France.
3rd series: (March 1986)

Three sets of three 2CV Dolly thus successively sold in March 1985, October 1985 and March 1986, but they actually offer seven different models.

Indeed, two models of the second series are renewed strictly identical gifts as part of the third.

Apart from the colors condoms which matches the color of the wings or to that of the body, the last two series have a cutting exactly the same color as the first series, each car has a different cutting.

2 CV Dolly receive a inner opening hood, wheels painted white Meije with hubcaps Dyane 6, two visor, sinkers of front turn signals and taillights supports black plastic and the 2CV 6 Charleston seats .

It seems that Dolly the third round have had seats in herringbone pattern.

March 1985

From March 21 is marketed a limited series called 2 CV Dolly 3 000 copies including 1500 for France.

Made on the basis of the 2CV 6 Special, it actually includes three models differing in two-tone dress.

The color combinations are available:

- Red Vallelunga EKB and gray cormorant TEUs.
- White and gray cormorant Meije EWT TEUs.
- Gray and yellow cormorant TEU Rialto EAA.

The seats are those of 2 CV 6 Charleston gray fabric in diamond patterns.

October 1985

Given the success of the first limited edition of the 2CV Dolly, Citroën launched the second of which 600 units are reserved for the French market where they are sold at a price of 34 200 F.

The color combinations are changed and it is now:

- Red and white Vallelunga EKB Meije EWT.

- Green bamboo and white AC 533 Meije EWT.

- Red and yellow Delage EKA Rialto EAA.

    (Bamboo Green receives no new color code).

March 1986

Citroën continues its momentum and markets a third and final limited series of three 2 CV Dolly at a price of 35 700 F.

The combinations available are:

- Red and white Vallelunga EKB Meije EWT.

- Red and yellow Delage EKA Rialto EAA.

- ELK night blue and yellow Rialto EAA.

2CV Cocorico

1986

The marketing of the limited edition of 1000 copies and only in France of the 2CV Kakariko based on 2CV 6 Special is done in 1986.

Senior White Meije EWT hue, this car gets on the sides of its body, except on the front fenders, a gradient from red to blue via white.

Sold 36,100 Francs, it receives benches lined Tep John's, known to be the least resistant of all 2CV linings marketed ever!

Last 2CV sold as part of a special series on the French market, the 2CV is designed by Serge Kakariko Gevin in January 1986 in anticipation of the World Cup Football, which takes place the following June and July .

While France advancing to the semi finals by eliminating Brazil after a penalty shoot memorable goal, Germany stands in his way and the adventure ends.

But the tricolor car so please Citroën that the decision is taken out of the still, after having cleared of stickers representing footballs, originally planned ...

This series thus celebrates the French spirit in general!

There was still copies for sale 6 months after its launch.

So she has not been a commercial success. France would have won the World Cup, the "Cocorico" would have been different and probably better sold.

2CV Chic

1986

Designed by Serge Gevin in 1986, among other special series of projects 2CV, the model called "2CV Chic" was not retained by Citroen.

It is therefore limited to a few sketches.

Serge Gevin, stylist Citroën service in 70-80 years, already author of Charleston, will consider other studies.

Twenty years later, Lucian Marin, passionate little Citroen, decided to make himself the project 2CV Chic, following an order from a friend.

Through documentation, very little detail must say, he manages his project materializes. Developed from a 2 CV 6, repainted gray Cormorant and white Meije, the 2 CV passes through the hands of two friends that reproduce graphic adhesives designed by Gevin. The result is remarkable.

2 CV runs a few months later, and the brother of Lucien falls in love, hence the construction of a second copy.

Bamboo 2CV

England

1987

The 2CV Bamboo is a specific model in the British market.

It will come out in 1987, during the last years of the 2CV.
Recognizable by its green hue of the same name (Bamboo), it will also
be used on special series Ente German-Grün and Sauss Ente.

2 CV Wella

England 1987

The Wella hair care company launched a competition in England for the release of a balm.

Among the items six specially prepared 2 CV. The operation is of course up in partnership with the local Citroen dealer that Leeds.

Of the six copies, won by the people of Yorkshire and surrounding counties, only one copy is still in circulation, the Mick Watson.

He bought the 2CV in 1989, responding to an advertisement in a local newspaper.

She was only 30,000 km on the clock.

Sauss 2CV Ente

Germany 1987

Produced by Citroen for Germany, the special series Sauss Ente just decorate the 2CV 6 without any changes.

Clearly stated in its logo with its speed acceleration "from 0 to 100km / h in 54.5 sec" Sauss Ente means "Duck which darkens."

The 2CV 6 602m3 is fastest with a top speed of 115 km / h.

All Sauss Ente 2CV exclusively Green Bamboo.

All other greens are personal achievements.

The wheels of the Sauss-Ente are white with black nuts, the bumper has plastic end caps (specificity German series) and the top is dark gray.

The Sauss Ente 2CV has a reversing light located under the rear bumper.

The duck drawn on the 2CV, with its leather helmet like the dark aviators a decided air towards the front of the car.

Inside, as on all German series seat is reclining.

The dashboard is that of 2CV Club, the counter is one of the friend 6 to brown background and the steering wheel is mono-branch.

It seems there have been nearly 400 Sauss 2CV Ente.

The last 2CV
1987/1990

The European anti-pollution standards and crash test requirements condemn the 2CV at the start of the 1990s.

Too expensive and not modern enough, it does not really coast with customers.

The production increased from 163,143 copies in 1974 to 54,923 in 1984.

The production ceases permanently in France February 29, 1988 at the plant in Levallois-Perret.

The traditional group photo to celebrate the end of an era. The 2CV left the assembly lines of the plant Levallois Perret February 29, 1988, after almost 40 years of production.

However, it will continue in Portugal Mangualde factory for a few years until the end of July 27, 1990 at 16h.

The final will be a Charleston Gray Cormorant bearing the serial number in the VF7AZKA00KA376002 kind.

July 27, 1990

After a parade 2cv6 Red Special, it's a big city with Charleston the serial number in the type VF7AZKA00KA376002.

2CV Cochonou

1997

The 2CV Cochonou the Tour de France do the show the old!

The Tour de France, real French institution as well as Camembert, sausage or ... the 2CV!

Such was the thinking of the advertising support of Cochonou project.

As an official supplier, he wants to stand out from the ambient banality. Thanks to their strength, 2CV could carry without problems kilos of sausages to distribute to cycling fans along the roads.

 With this idea, 13 years later the Cochonou 2CV know a hit on the turn and have even won a few awards such media prices or the favorite caravan tour of France.

Six cars, three 2CV sedans (including a limousine) and three 2CV vans (one pick-up).

Of course, these are the emblematic colors of Cochonou with lights, rims and yellow top and the rest of the body in imitation red and white gingham check of picnic tables.

In the van, a small AKS 400 in September 1972 did the trick.

A large basket, consisting of a large bun and a huge sausage reminds us of the spirit of ancient caravans of the large loop.

Indeed, the latter is more with a moderator and speakers mounted on the front bumper.

The sticker of heading accreditation the Tour de France is affixed on the left front fender and rear:

green for press vehicles, yellow for those of running, pink for the publicity caravan.

In its ranks, the team Cochonou 2CV Tour de France is fortunately endowed with "drivers-mechanics."

The latter, convinced deuchistes traverse France with good humor which one is a "victim" when driving 2CV ...

A smile here and a hello there, applause, thanks ...

But it's work!

At dawn, the mechanics proceed to final checks, astiquent bodywork and coolers are reloaded block for the next day.

Meanwhile, while the drivers make their way through the crowd, hostesses distribute public sausages and other promotional items.

There must be old nice car ...

The six 2CV are accompanied by a refrigerated semi-trailer, a truck 20m², three VIP vehicle, a moped and two rickshaws shaped before 2CV reduced to 80%.

And while cyclists ride 3500 kms, the 2CV them in 8500 swallow walkways and additional accommodation and forth between the race.

They must roll 6 or 7 hours straight at a speed of 30 to 40km / h. Of course, and this is a major feature of the tour of France, do not forget the mountains and other Alpine peaks!

In 2010, the pickup is aging and the little 2CV van loses its rural side.

She loses her wicker basket that will be attached to the roof of another car. The pickup then turns into a walking delicatessen, with the same success!

Some numbers :
390 mini sausages 000 and 1500 large cut a total weight 4t publicly offered in 3 weeks and 60 000 caps, bobs 15,000 and 15,000 scarves.

The commercial benefits are up.

The Tour de France cyclist affecting some 15 million viewers worldwide.

The race is broadcast on 118 television channels in 186 countries and through 75 radio stations, 398 newspapers and 100 websites.

2500 journalists are on site and nearly 12 million unique visitors are identified on the Internet.

Hermes 2CV

2008

Divine surprise on the Citroën stand at the World Auto 2008, in the midst of the 21st century concepts and models the manufacturer has not forgotten his past.

The C3 Pluriel Charleston is a nice nod to the ancestor, but it's even more exciting when it comes remake a person in lap, under an ultra-select livery, shared only with the Bugatti Veyron, excuse the bit:

a full range signed Hermes.

This will be the bicentenary of the 2CV, a Hermes 2CV for fifty years of national 2CV.

The car that lends itself to this beautiful staging is a 2CV6 1989 Special that takes a course exclusively brown paint, and typical of the famous saddle leather on the door trim, the ball of the gear lever, the rear view mirror and even the front driver's sun, luxury accessory if any.

For added elegance, the two seats are covered mid-Hermes canvas beige gray, mid-natural leather.

Finally, to complete this holding the hood and the lining of the inner body on the rear part of the vehicle are also upholstered in Hermes canvas.

On this occasion, the hood usually plastic, has been replaced by a fabric typically Hermes.

Two Headed 2CV

1950

The 2CV-called "two-headed", built by unit in 1950 at the request of firefighters Var was a valuable auxiliary Fire Brigade Cogolin for over ten years.

This vehicle was designed by the Departmental Inspector SDIS du Var, the Hourcastagné colonel, who, during a night of recognition made at the time with a 15 hp Citroen, being stuck in a mountain path and can turn around forced to turn back in reverse for several kilometers, guided only by a firefighter an electric lamp by hand.

Mr. d'Espinassy of Venel, President of the Union of forest owners at the time, held in Paris a research department to inventor patents.

These two men, aided by funds from the General Council of the Var, bought two semi-automatic clutch 2CV.

In a Paris workshop, workers were divided into two two 2CV.

They threw the back and welded fronts. The two parties are independent, each with a motor.

The four-wheel drive and directional. Along the position, the "rear" wheels are held upright with a square mounted on the steering column.

In all terrains and difficult passages, this vehicle can benefit, because the two motors, a first and a reverse although both engines are not under the same load. His code was Samba 54.

Being in the curious aspect of 2CV two heads welded to the other, the car thus has a pipe at the front and at the rear to the indifferently operate in both directions.

This machine allowed to conduct reconnaissance in the forest close to the fire.

Too long wheelbase and too low a floor made her unwieldy in all fields and especially in the mountains.

Moreover, the particular shape of this machine threw some confusion among motorists who were dubbed by it on the road.

All these reasons and the appearance of more modern equipment made this 2CV was withdrawn from service in the early 70s.

2CV A ambulance

1953

In November 1953, the coachbuilder Rouen Le Bastard has a 2 CV Ambulance he intends to propose to the surrounding municipalities with limited budgets.

It does exist, in all and for all, only one copy.

The gendarmerie 2CV

1954

The National Gendarmerie hit his first 2CV in 1954.

Seven years later, there was not a brigade on French territory who do not might dispose of at least a small Citroen.

Imagine the immense services that this little car went to the community for nearly thirty years.

Little Citroën has imposed immediately on his arrival in units in 1954, thanks to its qualities of maneuverability and handling allowing the military to evolve any time and on any coating, there including on snow.

Citroën 2CV had with a device particularly suited to rural France at the time.

This is why the Citroen Little was quickly dubbed by the gendarme who saw in it a perfect car "to do everything", it was also unquestionably.

2CV AU Police Relief Road

1954

In Paris in 1954 the motorcycle brigade is seen with several 2CV AU specially equipped to help the road users in need.

During the 1950s, the streets of major French cities are patrolled by the vehicle legendary font:

Type H Citroen. But from 1954, the first Parisian brigades receive 2CV, first AZ sedans then AZL since 1957.

The Parisian street brigade Chanoinesse located close to the police headquarters behind Notre Dame is a motorcyclist response unit.

The premises of this unit have an extensive workshop and have the capacity to accommodate bulkier vehicles than just motorcycles.

In 1953, Mr Gobin, Director of the Paris police decided to experiment with the commissioning of some cars in addition to motorcycles.

The test is performed with a 2CV van and the tests are conclusive. An order for 15 similar vehicles is launched and in 1954 they are three brigades will be equipped with AT 2CV Road Police Relief.

To ensure the pace, 15 drivers will be assigned to the task and ensured the following hours: 8am to 1:30 p.m. / 13h30-21h and 22h30-5h.

Each car consisted of two officials.

Each AT is made:

-A shortwave transceiver in association with the position of the prefecture which directs depending on traffic and the hot spots of the capital
-Of a radio for contact with other cars.

Every morning at 8am, they are at least 9 cars that are divided the capital into five sectors, through the most congested streets and intervening to free circulation.

But that's not all ... As the side panel of each 2CV:

"The crew of the vehicle's mission is to rescue you. If you need any help, make a sign to the driver immediately stop.

An official who is both engineer and rescuer is on board and will spontaneously to you. "

It is common for help a victim user to a puncture!

In the 1950s, the Parisian night experience sad hours of delinquency, 2CV AU will then often involved in arrests.

At night, the crews are equipped with 3 people instead of 2.

2CV in the army

2CV as a sedan or van, was for many years a liaison vehicle in the Metropolitan National Defense and Overseas.

The 2CV will coexist for some time with the famous US army jeep that will ultimately preferred him and his production will continue in France from 1955 to 1970 under license by Hotchkiss in Ornano plant in St Denis.

In the French Army, the 2CV van actually served in operations, including this very special edition revised and corrected by the study's offices GHAN1 (The Helicopter Group Carrier No. 1) of the Navy in heli-transportable version, and armed with a gun 75SR or 20 gauge.

War of Algeria

In 1955 gunships arrive in Algeria.

In 1956, the 31F flotilla of naval transports troops.

In 1957 it forms the GHAN1 with 32F and 33F: helicopter group naval air.

In 1959 Lieutenant Commander Eugene Peter Babot took command.

That same year he decided to turn a 2CV reinforced and air transportable pickup.

The 2CV is lighter and much lighter than the jeep.

It removes, cutting all that is unnecessary adds anchor points for transport under helicopter puts a mid-heavy armament.

First a barrel 57 mm recoilless, the same that was used on scooters Vespa / Acma and a gun 75 mm recoilless.

The vibrations caused by the fire will give up such weapons.

Another weapon is tested, the barrel 20mm MG 151 cannon.

The 2CV is named Julius, radio call of Babot.
It is top secret, hence the few existing pictures.

Picasso 2CV

Andy Saunders, amateur of contemporary art, set out to achieve a "real" Citroen Picasso to make real tribute to the master of surrealism.

He spent 6 months of life to change a 2 CV so cubism.

The inspiration came from the portrait of Dora Maar him which he took over the assortment of colors and the particular anatomy reviewed by Picasso.

Andy Saunders said he was convinced that the choice would be between Pablo Picasso Picasso's 2CV and the Xsara and C4 of the French manufacturer.

After its transformation into art (sic!), The car was homologated (England) for the road to be used daily.

For indicators, he (Andy Saunders), stated that he had to use the hand (so Gaston) the driver's side (right here) because the two were flashing on the left!

He fought on selling his work at the Center Pompidou or the Tate Gallery in London.

He felt, as a work of art, to 1 million pounds ... but nevertheless admitted that if these institutions refused to buy him, he would be forced to put it on consignment from a vendor automobile!

He finally put in an auction organized by RM Auctions in London **WITHOUT RESERVATION**, Wednesday, October 29, 2008 ...

It was estimated between £ 10,000 and £ 14,000 ... and was sold £ 8,800 !!!

wooden 2CV

2017

The creator of the artwork called Michel Robillard, a retired cabinetmaker.

After several years of work, 5 exactly, he assembled the 2CV on a base Dyane 6 of 1966 still taking up the chassis, engine and tires + rims on a classic 2CV.
For the first time, the wooden 2CV rolled!

"The goal was to make it roll since it is a first in France.

I think today I have achieved my goal "

Visit poster's website welcomed our cabinetmaker whose "dream is to roll this car at the foot of the Eiffel Tower."

The work of art has required different woods: pear for the framework, apple for the bonnet, the walnut for the wings and the steering wheel, the cherry for the doors and the trunk of the elm for mangy the dashboard.

The 2CV cinema

Can not put all the appearances of 2CV

The most famous cult scenes of the 2CV

"The Sucker"

Production Year: 1964

Release date: March 1965
Directed by Gérard Oury
With Bourvil, Louis de Funes, Venantino Venantini.

The film 2CV
"The Sucker".

Les Gendarmes in St Tropez

Saga The Gendarme of St Tropez
Release Date: October 6, 1982
Directed by Jean Girault, Tony Aboyantz
Louis De Funès, Michel Galabru

French movie.
Genre: Comedy
Duration: 1h 35min.
Production Year: 1982

Contents

A Romain & Eva

.

Printed in Great
Britain
by Amazon